A MIDWESTERN INTROVERT'S ATLAS

POEMS

JAKE GRIGGS

Rocket Science Press
SHIPWRECKT BOOKS PUBLISHING COMPANY
Winona, Minnesota

Cover and interior design by Shipwreckt Books.
Cover concept by Jake Griggs.

Shipwreckt Books Publishing Company
357 W. Wabasha Street
Winona, Minnesota 55987

Library of Congress Control Number: 2026941978

ISBN: 979-8-9944316-1-0

For Sara, Hayden, and Åsta.

Contents

The Inner Passage

In a Dream with My 6—year—Old Self

He came to me in the middle of a pasture
Reached up and held my hand
We smelled the blooming irises
We explored the abandoned barn
We looked at a book of postcards and pictures
One was of a hillside with 500 antlered deer
He pointed and explained the nature of things
How the landscapes were once barren
How bones can look like orange strings
How the deer looked like horses
And how each horse is uniquely itself
I got up to say goodbye
He smiled and said, *my heart is a lonely horse too.*

I Want to be a Poet

but none of these words
are mine. I don't conquer fear

with a mouth of constellations.
The veins in my wings
are not flowing rivers.

I am not a second moon
made of water and gas,
though I rise and fall too.

I am part of the glowing
shoal, the collective, one
of many bough stuck petals,

dark and drenched.
I exist, yes, but
I'm not a dying star.

I was told that life demands
quiet bravery. So, I seek peace
among the wild, and never cease

my exploration. Some day
I'll open and bloom and speak
my own words into the air. Become

a never—ending forest
where fallen trees are seen
and heard, even if no one is there.

Heirlooms

We sort piles of items, charms
and old photos, random faded boxes
full. Parts of the past, soon mine.

One soft zippered case holds my mother's
jewelry. We carefully untangle the necklaces
and search for the earring pairs.

Mostly plated. Mostly costume. Mostly
free of consequence. A certain strand
stands above the rest, simple

and unassuming. Brilliant blue beads,
small washers of gold, and pearls
in alternation. Pieces rare, arranged and orderly.

We find the tiny matching
earrings, which display unity
through shape and color.

I am told these were purchased
from a corner shop jeweler in Tehran.
There are a few other artifacts

throughout the house that commemorate
those times; a tapestry bold with maroon
blue, and gold. A brass chafer urn. Arabic

stickers on a trunk. I turn a pearl in my fingers.
My truths from those times are the grain
at the center, covered by calcified layers

of life, who's iridescence distracts. In the pearl
is the milk I fed to our spaniel, an entire
week's worth, and the ire I received from my father

for the deed. The perfectly round
heaven stones of lapis lazuli dot the chain
like the kindnesses I remember; the old woman

in a chador, face covered, a robed angel
offering me a coke when the
bus broke down. Or the Tehrani boy

I played with on the concrete floor
of his home, rugs adorning the walls.
And that dry ultramarine sky, resonating

like the turban worn by Vermeer's
girl with a pearl earring. I wonder if
my mother received a jeweler's magnificent

smile? The gold is bright between
the stones when we pay attention
to the metal, soft and precious with detail.

As we place the wonders back
in their pockets, Mom talks
of the people we knew who were killed.

Of how we barely made it out. Of
the things I never knew, oppressed
or forgotten. Amid the collections

of my life there are treasures
to find, even in the domains
of dictated violence. Someday

my mother will go, and when that time
arrives, I will be left to hold
these stories in a strand and know

how splendor can come from all places.

January Porch Reminders

In the cold surgical air
Past the reach of sun
A wolf moon full of emptiness passes
The earth is a muscle sheathed in silver skin
Beauty confined under cold layers
Lit but faint, for now contained
Visible when stripped back to the fiber
Instead of moving under a dark hide of stars
Raw in the night
All waits, impatient for spring
Remember, remember
Do not push or seek to find
Search to fill
Want nothing
Except nothing

Another Person's Treasure

At your request I'm cleaning the van, an Oxpecker in a hippo's mouth. I move a seat to find a stash of stale cereal, most of it reduced to dust. One or two gold rings remain hard and intact, artifacts of a distant past. A vacuum hose in hand, I'm about to do what's easy, like asking you to throw away the contents of a tote filled with first grade homework, stored in the attic for years. The wind picks up and sweeps an old receipt from the back seat, across the lawn, tumbling away. Somehow, a decade ago, you knew each piece was precious, paper marked moments that blew past us. Cute poems and hand scrawled animals drawn on stacks of old math. Parchment from a time when our children filled their pockets full of dandelions, acorns, and interesting rocks, collections from walks in the woods. In the whirring whine of white noise, a suction pulls me back into the late May sun. Before I fly to new chores, I switch off the machine. Put the seat back in place. Leave the Cheerios safe underneath.

I Drove Through the Fog and Was Left Holding Her Coat

My wife woke at 5 a.m. with barely a breath.
On the swift wings of a Dakota owl
hollow silent bones moved
to clutch and lift her
higher, towards the heavens,
over time, smaller, and smaller,
until only a fleck remained.
Voices became whispers.

I was heavy on the pedal,
driving fast to help her,
winding down the highway
and crossing the river.
A nurse took her upon arrival
behind hospital doors.
She departed in pain.
So did I, walking
head down to the car.
The sky hung low.
The rain swelled.
Ravines ran.

I thought of the basket in the kitchen
that holds refills and new scripts.
The voided orange bottles are filled
to keep her rhythm and breathing strong.
Keep my spirit afloat.
Maybe those bottles are just more
empty space in the world.

One day her body.
On that day, my core.
Perhaps nothing will be full again.
I will clear out her dressers,
and memories of her will diminish.
Even the moon, in solidarity,
will fast on occasion,
diving into darkness.

Shocked, I sat by myself in the parking lot
and thought about our old gray cat.
It hissed at shadows,
a little crazy and mean,
but not to me.
We had to put it down
after the tumor set in.
I knew all those years
it was busy dying. Daily,
I gave it what was needed.
Love and a little sustenance.

I snapped back and the wipers swished,
clearing the windshield
to help me see the road ahead,
mind twisting with the asphalt.
Truths travel many paths,
even that of death.
Its paradox, death's paradox, comes
when one hears its name.
It happened to me on
a day I nearly drowned.
I found at the edge of known gloom

everything is greener, brighter.
From that brink there are times
the drug of death brought me
closer to life. Closer to all days,
clear and crisp, before leaves turn,
before stalks brown and curl.
I'd like to believe
when the scythe swings
everyone has a choice. Ride the dragon
of pity and spite, or
embrace hope and joy like a balm.
I wish the latter for her,
behind the white doors.
I hope she is guided
to the purest medicine. No counters
to navigate over. Just an aura
that permeates and takes her aches
away. Brings her back fully
to her people and laughter.

Back home, in the crushed rock driveway,
I exit the car and take my time.
Autumn colors are scattered on the lawn
and trees look half—dead in the rain.
As I stare at the bare dark branches, a certain
optimism takes root. The maple helps me know
what is possible. That it will begin anew
after the ice has come and gone.
A steady pour soaks my shoulders.
I go inside. Housebound with my thoughts,
I decide to clean the shower.
In the corner are clumps

of long hair, piled like
raked leaves.
How can any be left?

The hair in my hand brings me
to a threshold. I recognize that
time advances regardless of legs,
skin, or skeleton. It matters not,
the means, diagnosis, or
the unseen shaving of time.
With my pets.
                    With my people.
All I can do is give love
and a little sustenance.
And despite every intention,
despite my best efforts,
I can't stop nature.
When the veil is drawn and
I see raw mortality,
as pieces of my clan expire, I dissipate too.
I call on myself to muster the fortitude
to grieve.

Follow me.
When the sky breaks and I see the sun setting,
I'll place all my thoughts of unfairness, and
anger, and any bitter, bitter words,
and pack them alongside my platitudes
in a shoebox with a bouquet of baby's breath
to bury in the back yard of my heart
where the daffodils will bloom
in the warming spring soil.

Cyrtanthus Ventricosus

When your days are ablaze with bills to pay, and hate fuels hate, while the weather whips frenzy after frenzy, and friends fade or pass away, comfort is a mirage where we may never arrive. All may seem hidden or lost or charred or buried or gone. In times like those hope feels audacious. Yet the red—orange reality of the fire lily exists. It pushes through soot to face the sun. Rise from your ashes and realize that you have purpose you don't always understand, and that you are also capable of surviving the fire to color your world, a harbinger of grasses to come …

A Body of Water is a Functional Depression

I traveled to a great distant lake
On the way I crested a hill then descended
Kettle range somewhere behind me
                                        Lizard back bumps in the distance

That was yesterday
I'm now at the foot of a bay
Watch the kingbirds skip from branch to branch
The rolls of surf curling to shore
A rhythm, a heart
Stones lapped for ages in the waves
In the beats I loosen my being
Give myself to the water's horizon
My worries, broken shells at my feet
Amongst the morning spiders I feel my sprockets lock
My gears turn slow
To watch the world wake
                                        Pendulum of the day
In motion, changing

In the grip of utter peace I hear sound beyond sound
Tune in to the frequency conflict makes
Amid echoes of war
I open my duffel of sorrows
Diffuse them in the drowse of dawn
In through the nose, out the mouth
Try to quiet my mind
Perform a ritual of examination
I search for joy in these spaces

Even the kingbirds stop to watch
I rediscover a truth
There is beauty all around
In fact, it's all that's left
A thought that causes a swell
Each moment a colorsplashed view
Light to shine through a thin sealed eye

Still, a shadow of sorts is my companion
Tied to my limbs and life
It hides in the dark, constant
In fact, it's how darkness is made
I feel immense cavities
Where I know my happiness should go
How can sand fully fill the sea
How do I stuff the sky with down
How can I breathe the universe
The swish of the shore swings me around
I have absolutely nothing
Knowing even my palms are empty
Why do I have such trouble
With my grip and with letting go

Let me say it here, plain, without muzzle or metaphor
I am bound by a sadness I cannot name, though I try

It flows bottomless like deep pockets of water
What say the Tao about that
The dimensions of dark and darker
That water is unmoving in the cold

It clings in the air of heat
Either way I'll have trouble breathing
Please let me melt and dissipate
Sink into the soil or evaporate and float away
The spiders and I fathom a lack of satisfaction
The struggle is existence
Existence is a struggle
I dredge my memory for answers
When did I learn to swim

And I dredge deeper to find desire in the muck
A cup of coffee
A new car
A nice house
Love from someone unwilling or unable
The return from death of a dear one
The replenishing of nature and earth
I have been raised my whole life to strive
But what if my desire is to be free from desire
What if what I want
Is less

I shift in my chair
Ears to the air for answers
The lake speaks, I listen
It says,

Do not sit idle like I
Find that which sustains and do it
Keep it close
Let it make space between you and your shadow
Allow it to protect

Leave all things behind
Bear no apologies
Be curious, and open, and willing to change
Because change will inevitably come
And with it a chance at rapture
Let it
Let it alter your banks but not zones
Different, yes
But a sea is only itself once
And hands which are free
Are hands that may help

The waves slowly cull themselves
In the shade of a branch over water
A fish rises nearby
Not a breath of wind exists
A dragonfly lights on my arm
Born on the water now living in air
Subtractive colored wings of translucence
With veins that flow like roadmaps
Does it see me or see through me
Can it sense a light inside
Are we strangers
Before I pull the last sip from my mug
I clear my throat
Whisper to more than myself
Embedding *I'm here* for the larvae to recognize
Words to ripple across the water

This bay could be any bay
Sturgeon, Hudson, Tampa, or Ha Long

It could be one of Pigs or Paradise
Regardless of place or salinity
It speaks the same language
But it's done talking now
The kingbirds move on
The spiders all hide
The dragonfly left only its current
I center my breath and I rise from my seat
To make my coffee cup clean

Looking Skyward in the Courtyard on a Fifteen Minute Break

I drove over a river to get here. I will cross it again
when I leave, but that's still in the distance.

Stepping away and away, outside
of the color—temperature controlled
zones, sliding glass doors,
single—serve café machines,
and empty whiteboards, I sit on the cold brick of a long retaining wall.

A reprieve from the open concept office
and far from the watchful eye of a webcam,
my atrophied cells crave to be moved away
from the rote responses of reflexive greetings.

I think of when I last smiled, sitting
in this same spot I don't know
how many months ago, amid blooming
coneflower, watching sparrows scuffle
over a lone scrap of bread
when they were all bested
by a fat gray squirrel.

No days until anything, and missing
the days from. Its unidentifiable
except for daily routines;
I am long beyond the counting of days.

The same coffee, same creamer, same

amount of sugar to make it palatable.
The same cobwebs in the spaces
that don't move, even if the spiders have changed.
The same framed faces memorialized on the walls.

Maybe I'm an exhibit on display
for some other entity, left
in a large enough enclosure
not to notice
the outer walls or fences.

I open my lungs
and breathe for the first time today,
feeling the stretch in my chest.
I know the rot that resides there; not *true* rot.
Not meat left out and spoiled, not
the bratty child talking back to his father
in blind defiance, not the cut that is red
and festering, not the softening wood center
of a century old maple; but an unseen disconnection
from importance and self—worth, a blackening disposition,
a decomposition of the soul.

Sitting at the edge of the late summer grass
with my head slightly tilted, I look up to see what looks back.
I spy a high circling speck. An opaque
figure cutting around clouds, riding
thermals, doing what it does, winding
down, wings wide in a processional glide down;
down to what it can smell.

It cleans the carcasses of the dead. I know this ugly bird.
Turkey vultures prepare bones for their next life.

I sniff the arm of my clothes. Maybe the scent
of my despair is too much to pass up;
more specters appear, and one becomes three,
honing their stained beaks, letting
my spirit fill their senses.

I squint, smile. I want these merciful birds
to coast close, settle near, hop over and rip
away the bad pieces, take my aches,
loose me from my decay, fill
their gullets with my carrion and consume
the worst parts of me; eat the meat
that is dormant and dead, so we both can live.

When I view these wraiths
as they cascade to the places
they're called, I'd like to think that all the people
and the sparrows
and the spiders
and the squirrels
and the flowers
and the Mississippi,
anything with eyes or a head,
would know to bow in silent reverence
as they witness the transcendence among them.

Before I stand and go,
I shut my eyes and comply. In that dark
I see them spiral closer.

A Partial List: A Year of Notes Dictated to My Phone

My mothlike thoughts skitter
Pop past lights
Clink and bounce around your glass
Pheromones, your stare
Shadows soon swallowed by night
Like a whispered word, close your eyes
I'll fly past your mauve sky
Seek your kiss in the edgeless gradation

∞

A day without change is not one fully lived. We cannot control our opportunities or environments. Only our preparedness for them.

∞

The perfect imperfections on a Painted turtle shell

∞

The crux of my quandy is like bedroom floor laundry
It's not dirty or clean, but something between
Column A, column B, you solemnly see
That answers lie outside the norm

∞

I walk through the verdant gates and the leaves become me

∞

12' wide
8' long
7'10" high
2'2" deep

∞

How much of myself must I destroy to find inner beauty?

∞

Call Hokah Oil

∞

Thoughts picking up so much speed
They create a spark
Friction in the open air
Soon I'm consumed by flame

∞

I floated so far, and so long, I can't see your shores anymore.

∞

I have relationships that I don't expect you to understand
I'm not asking you to follow where I'm going

∞

Remember reading for April 4

∞

The older I get the less interested I am in documenting my experiences, and the more interest I have being present in them.

∞

Sunny side up allows for a richer plate.

∞

A body in motion, adrift in the astral abyss…

∞

A parade of ugly things at the airport:

—Special lanes to separate the "cream" on the same carpet to board a plane.

—The sneering gentleman in first class who refused to have his overhead used.

—The loud woman making a phone call via speaker.

—One man crushing another's bag to make room for his own.

—Unbuckling when you shouldn't, leaving your phone in regular mode, acting like rules don't apply.

∞

Fescue

∞

How many lonely desolate souls exist under this same sky?

∞

We must not give in to our gloom
The glint of ghosts show
Loneliness doesn't belong to you or me
It's a collective possession
We are family through our hurt and despair

∞

Plus 90 days until it's fully out of the system —1 day to month in blood.

∞

There seem to be a lot of self-important motherfuckers around.

∞

Help me quit hiding myself
Stop covering my life's gemstones
With the dust of grief
Collect and polish
Turn them, turn them
Release their gleam
Make them shine again

∞

The world is a puzzle the sections of an orange. We search for the packets that fit.

∞

Those with rusty belts may have dirty hearts.
May the American dream rest in peace.

∞

The most beautiful thing we can do is tell the truths we know in our marrow.

We can't help but be drawn to the fires that will ignite us.
So we wander the countryside in search.
I'm just a weary traveler, like everyone else, trying to fix the deep fissures in my soul.
That I exist at all, that this reality is here, is miraculous.
If I am living a dream for some other being,
I'll try and be happy doing it.

∞

The Blues are my mountain.

∞

Out on the porch enjoying the full moon, fireflies, stars and a cold beer. The breeze is out of the north tonight, which means the interstate to my south is silent. Just crickets and other night creatures and the occasional ghostly moan of a train several miles away following the river down the valley, and suddenly I've never had the urge to hop the rails more than I do at this moment.

∞

I can be strange sometimes because I don't know my place.

∞

Is it tragedy, or is it poetry? The fact that none of this really matters. The fact that the only thing that does matter is this moment. What we do and how we feel right now. Is there anything truly more poetic?

∞

Providence

∞

You don't see the chronically sick kidneys, or the paper skin that decorates her body, or the buried scars in the crooks of her arms. No gauge is visible to show there will never be 100% again. Or even 80. Those numbers might as well not exist. Even the sound of them lights an anger that is tired of explaining itself. Always tired. The gloss of her eyes is a sadness that pools. Fool all of us into believing it's her vigor and zest for life.

∞

The great instability

∞

I'm not looking for affirmation, argument, or agreement; I just want y'all to know that I love Huey Lewis and The News. Always have.

∞

It's hard to see myself when I'm my own ghost.

∞

Check on Mom and Dad.

∞

It is here in this space, this thicket of my mind, that I must find my own solace and peace. My own perfection and joy. If I can accomplish this, then right living is at hand. We are meant to be alone, together. Siblings in emptiness. A citizen of our own inner space.

∞

Paul at the State Office

∞

The memory of your scent buried in my brainstem. Pockets of air in bread. Vanilla on my skin.

∞

If you want to believe in something, believe in asters. Those small purple blossoms that push forward through the brown and fading grass. They give us glimpses of what is to come after winter. They are the hope we need.

∞

I should not allow my burdens to be yours.

∞

Wheels pressed into cut wheat
My life is full of emptied shells

∞

I'm lying on the hard earth discovering what I know, veracious. That I've only truly loved once, that my children will need to save themselves, that my own salvation will come from learning to want less, to breathe more, to offer myself to the sky. I have gifts to extend if I can only better understand my own awkwardness and ill timing. I am nobody's savior, but I can still allow others to be seen amid their struggles and suffering. My only authentic desire is the same as many others. To love and be loved. Everything else is ephemeral. Like this grasshopper on my knee, now gone. I must learn from him. To lighten my load. Not punish myself for mistakes. Have internal faith and love. Trust my own legs and jump.

∞

What are your beacons? Call them by name.
Light them. Let their fire be seen.

∞

Hello. My name is Jake. I'm here on behalf of the creatives. For all the believers and dreamers and anyone who's ever made something out of nothing.

Riffing on Clouds

Let the mind fly like a curious kid, look up high, do what I did
The clouds stacked across the sky like a jazz drum, like cotton blue hair, candy honeydew juicy drops
Like spiderwebs, old church heads, misty gorilla rosin cloth
Like fluffy sheep, eel meat, mildew stained grape leaf
Like frosty foamy bubbly beer, people, state, animal, sheets, a fucking fire breathing dragon
Like powdered sugar, bearded Santa, angel fluff at Christmas time
Like marshmallow, like a sudsy tub, like the fur of a two—week kitten
Live Venus, like Titan, like the grey matter, like the tail of a comet streaking through, past Neptune
Like seafoam, tree seeds, puffs of dust leading down paths I can't see
Like aphid spit, quiet fire pits with dead rabbits, and a bright camera flash makes the scene lit
Like a baby's wet wipe or grandma's cataract eyes
And there's no thunder
No thunder
No crack and smash
No thunder
Gray.   Strings.   Blew.
Split milkweed pods, and the silver strands turned cobalt
The easy exhale from clove cigarettes, early morning haze as it drifts over valleys
Unclarified butter in the sky, seared tuna sliding in your jaws, rubies on the inside
Shorn wool, lanolin, strange spots between freckles trapped on your skin

Waiting on the specter of the sun to stop hiding, to come out and give me a kiss
Shape shift and maker, partial erasure, like the steams from your anger, or my unfulfilled dreams
Tomorrow's promise or today's waking life changing, drifting, never the same
It's just me in the car barreling down a road I swear I've been on before
Riding into the rays and I breathe …
And I squeeze …
And I breathe

During a Summer of Record Temps and Endless Canadian Smoke

Standing at midday in a field of tall grass during the first clear afternoon in weeks, I look up at the clouds. I wonder where they come from and where they're going. Are these the seeds that will create water on Earth? I look across at the peonies and imagine sand dollars at their feet. I walk through the yard, as is my want, among the tall trees that line the drive. The sun stains the leaves with a mosaic that vibrates, a walnut's verdant canopy, a kaleido of emeralds above. One cannot see this from space, from some passing satellite in the sky that will continue unblinking after all mankind is erased —when bits of blacktop may still be visible, beside what's left of the rivers, and our violent seas. The orbiting machines will gaze down long after we're gone. In the daylight there is no sign of them now. I would be alone but for the crackling of gravel. A vehicle approaches. I squint in the bright afternoon at my grown child pulling in the driveway. I remember looking down at him sprawled on the carpet pushing toy cars with his hands. He shuts off the engine and emerges to shout, *What's for dinner?* and I think about the meat simmering in the crock, and who's turn it is to clean up, and what tomorrow may bring, and his entire life laid out in one long string. And everything beyond. I think of all the fathers to come and how they may also marvel at the beauty and barrenness of our existence, as the temperatures slowly creep up and up, and we recede, and all else fades. Which of us will apologize to our children for bringing them into this world?

As I walk back to the house, I'm careful not to step on the splendid and soft purple flowers of clover that grow from my ineptitude. A Rubythroat zips by to sip from the hostas. This moment exists, and will never again, and the thought of it makes me want to tear with the joy of holding it all close. My son makes his way up the steps. I ruffle his hair.

We smell the charred earth.
We go inside together.

Fibonacci Unwinding

I gathered wood for our decorative fireplace, collecting
some brittle paper birch, cut last year for a timber stand
improvement project on state land, and unknowingly
carried with me the foreign seed of delicious garlic
mustard —invasive, pungent and sweet, now covering
my yard in a spring snowfall of small white petals, a
terminal dust.

Days away a train derails and spills the toxin of progress in
East Palestine, leaving Norfolk Southern with the best of
bad options; burning vinyl chloride near water that
snakes through yards and orchards.

I used an AI program today for the first time and it felt
comfortable and wrong, wearing the slippers of god.

Everything costs more, yet the line at Starbucks never
seems to get shorter.

How many chances do we get at this?

I can't keep it straight.

Please help me.

Infinite? One?

Or

zero.

An Invitation to Commune on My Front Porch

Upon watching the sunset of my 49th year,
in the mauve and purple parallax,
low clouds to high, exists the line
between vertigo and clarity. As they pass
I'm reminded of watching the Boundary
Waters shore, trees from a canoe
as they floated against their backdrop,
leaves crafting careful turns,
ballerinas on branches, alive now
as they were then
by virtue of memory's deep frames.
I stand on a platform and realize
we move at speeds we can't see.

The yotes yap across the valleys,
owls are taking roll call,
and the Junebugs are awake and a'buzzin
while I watch the flower moon
rise and bloom.
Listen to the toads trill songs nearby
and feel the dewpoint creep in without asking.
Why is it the closer we get to our raw origins,
our vicious and unforgiving truths,
this wild and untamed earth,
that we also get closer to alleviating our anxieties,
a chance to be present with contentment,
to cozy up to ourselves
and cuddle under a quilt of peace?
I wink at the high silky cirrus

and babble a billion points of illumination
made pale by the lunar light,
feeling inescapably small,
still, I persist,
exhale stardust and twist my head slightly
to watch the pine boughs sway and dip,
dancing to the beat of the early summer air
to the point that I wonder who's leading
and who's following.
After you, my dear.

I don't want to live another day without this.
Hell, I don't even want to go to sleep
if it means I get to drink more of this
in long slow pulls, a joyful saturation.
If you're still here,
sit with me a minute.
Dear reader, set down your fears.
Take off your worries.
Hang your hate on the tiny hook it deserves
and just sit. Rock a chair and listen.
If only for a moment,
grow older with me.
Explore these wonders in my company
while the world changes stations or fitfully sleeps.
Let it seep deeply under your skin, yes,
into your human xylem and confess, yes,
to the endless darkness how good it feels and, yes,
how much we all need to return and connect
with what has always been there,
always alive,
always waiting.

Though I have no authority
or expertise other than the days I've lived,
I ask for your belief when I state
that the nebula of consciousness
will possess us if we let it, if we loose
our fear of being unmoored,
enveloped by a lack of confinement.
Though it is scary, let go. Float.
Let the wind, or the universe,
or whatever gods may be take us
on a moonlight cruise deep through
the river of the mind,
leaving our bodies quaking and trembling,
chock full of excitement and awe.
I'll hold your hand past rapids of asteroids
and starfalls and ripples of time.
As it takes me, it will take you.
If we can drift a moment
in that space between,
that liminal bliss, therein lies all we desire.
In the air where a barn swallow dips.
In the ribbon of water hiding rainbows.
In the quiet whisper of a cool norther breeze.
The faint, steady beat of our hearts.

Blowing Out Birthday Candles

I wish I could bundle
All of your hurt and anxiety
Carry it to arid planes
Carefully unfold it all
And leave it to dry
Until it's brittle and thin
Then use it as kindling
To light your pyre
So you can attract the beings
That know your light
As something they simply must be near
Because it fills them
With the warmth and hope
Of humankind

Tephra Fall Zone

To Dive

I watched the boy from afar
Tiptoe to the edge
Teeter and peek over
His ache to jump apparent
As he stood, hands clasped
Arms tight to his chest
Knees together, slightly bent
Coiled —afraid
I tried to tell him to relax
Be loose
Let yourself fall
You might jump in later, braver
But letting yourself go
Into the unknown
Is an exhilaration
Only put there by love
And impossible to replace

Dormant

I heard a story
After a hundred snows passed
A house was razed
Where it once stood
Scraped from the earth
Foundation and all
Soil shy to the sun
Began to produce

From the vacant space
Up sprouted and grew
A new compass plant
Not beheld by earth
For generations
It stretched for the sky
Awake from slumber
Turned petals pale
Into the sunshine
After all that time
It only wanted
To bloom

Sometimes my seeds
Are spread before me
And I build on top of them
For ease of concealment
Or my own careless haste
No one knows they exist
Except me (and now you)
Perhaps when I'm bolder

I'll destroy the structures
That are empty and cold
So my heart can take root
And grow

An Offering

I leave a basket of myself
To be discovered
Contents carful and true
Pieces of my being nestled neatly
A cribbage board, bourbon
The scar on my brow
Cupid's high school bow
And harsh things prior to
Fifteen too

This basket weave, a wonder
Perhaps observing the vessel is enough
But if one chooses to pry open
Such wicker
Expose delights within
Embrace the human heart
The lid may be closed again
But never forgotten

My sweet vermouth
I am dark firewater
I bring a cherry
And a grin
Gaussian warmth
Soft at the edges

Bud

Alone, small
Time spent packed
In compressed layers
Of dense anxiety
Kept and hidden
Unaware of your worth

Unwrap, uncoil
Feel vulnerable
Let the lavender permeate
Join colorways that amaze
Don't hold—break open
Roll your sepals back
Peel and bloom
Permit the peace
Give yourself to the field; exist

Muse

Let me paint from the dark shocks
Pushing the hues and chroma
Fill my canvas

Let optimism strike bright on string
Build cheerful sound
To enwrap my essence

Let laughter guide my stones
Build respectful foundations
With footings deep down

Let beams illuminate a stage
Where I can spin and project
Entertain my thoughts

Let my cutlery dice and fillet
Infuse with spice and soul
A feast of grandeur

Let it all run through me
Rivulets into words
Permit me to feel mana within

For You Who I Cannot See

For you who I cannot see
Know that I receive your notes
Clicks and chimes become lonely smiles
Beats quicken in anticipation
My flame floats a ballet with your whispers
I hear you

For you who I cannot see
Lay bare your buoyant joy
Pull me from the doldrums
Leave me in wonderment
Is your fragrance vanilla or petrichor?
I breathe you

For you who I cannot see
But for pain and glass
Your stories passed still rare
I dream a feast to cure dark hearts
Between sips of noir
I taste you

For you who I cannot see
Yet make my Delmonico Cystal sweat
Ears hot and neck
My foot bounces with a nervous verve
To a soft reverie of blue velveteen
I feel you

For you who I cannot see
I lay this at your steps

For thoughts, invisible
Buds beneath never break
I responsibly resist, your eyes
Don't disclose

—I'm yours.

Genesis

The gradients of first light slowly expose
the weathering of a barn overgrown.
A creek eddies, bending 'round rock and earth
right next to long shadows cast by young trees.
Cottonwoods flash like a canopy of spoons
above the humus and litter afoot.
Descry a child with a genuine smile
as a dragonfly consumes its catch.

Beauty under sol
            above the mantle
                        in paradox.

An amphibious serenade late in the day
is the prelude to fields of rain-soaked ripe oats.
Fingers and beaks prepare to retire
as the red berries ripen to black.
The quick flash of firelight splashes nearby
while the moon wanes and claws its way up.
And as the far howls rejoice over sweet carrion,
two people embrace in a kiss.

Conceptions of Passion

I.
In this pitch of ink
these symbols and characters
are the rabbits I've brought
and left soft at your feet.

II.
I attempt the absurd
to explain the inscrutable.

My words turn carnal,
ferine, innate.

I ignite
with the warmth

of a molten limerence.
You must know

your love and touch
are not wants.

They are needs.

III.
Beyond sunrise, sunset–
                                        be the celestial fire
that burns me,
                                        the radial waves,
the coronal mass attraction

that passes my atmosphere
and lights my aura
with your aurora,
flashes of white,
of green,
of crimson,
deep into my sulci,
blind me
with your luminance.

IV.

Like the great bell's reverberation,
you summon vibration
deep in my marrow,
my pneuma, the dancing
eyes, open lilium of my heart.

V.

Like a brush
loaded with oil,
ready to expend its chroma,
smear on canvas,
spread wide
with broad strokes,
your Klimt,
my Flöge,
the touch of two hands
in creation.

VI.

A late summer pear,

pearly teeth

sliding past skin,

into tender flesh,

juice dribbling down chin,

sustain me.

VII.
Like a lake of attraction,
          you are my loch.

I thirst and pine to drink,
          an anxious anticipation of you

laving my lips,
          tongue utterly flush.

Let me sip your blood-warm water,
          wade farther from shore,

where I make my devotion,
          where boundaries mix,

where my heat becomes your heat,
          and the viscus, smooth tension

apprehends us both,
          rendering everything wet.

VIII.
You, my corporeal urges,
my somatic comfort,
my anthesis,

my ether, my ground,
my wild and shaking cosm.
Be pleased

with my whisper,
my kiss,
my breath a zephyr on your neck,

fresh with love
and desire
and love.

IX.
As you have in my caverns,
allow me to ignite a blaze
that will glow giant and red,
and enter a space
where the external world
is left dead
for a time.

X.
Let us return.
            Let us bask.
                        Let us rest.

Let us share an understanding
        that those moments can be
                meteorites that streak the sky

whether cloudy or clear,
        pheromones that call
                all wild creatures forward.

Let us hear through the silence,
        without remark,
                let us reach out,

and find each other.
        Draw close, connect
                in the dark.

Sleep Talking

Slumbering love,
my words for you float in the night—
        slip and fall:
  The three-week blaze of a tamarack
        drops its dress,
   bones exposed,
only to cover them once more.

Looking East at 1am

I can't sleep, and I imagine you're up
Mood light on as the tears
                                        drop
Perhaps living in a song
    Or lost in an image
                        I yearn to tag along
                                        a sponge of thoughts
                                I send mental twine
                                        to tie to your door
                                so that I may trace
                                                the rough twists
                                with fingertips
                        through the blind eve
                                        to be with you
Push eyes past this page
                        through words into and
                                                out of your breath
                        A subtle rise in your chest
                                with eyes that desire to shut
What do you do in these wee hours
                                when all else is asleep?
                                Do you drift … awake
                                        waiting for wards
of slumber?
                        You know
                                        flowers
                                                like
                                        yourself
                                that bloom and display
                        all day,

they need to stop
and rest
too …

Unrequited

The forest bares its spirit in the winter
Stark branches cold
Nothing to hide
Searching for strength to tell us again

Every leaf a love letter
Started in spring
Finished in summer
Forgotten at the end of each fall

Lesson of the Heart

I laid out my emotions
Raw, unrefined
And saw they could not stay
So, I rolled them up
And looked for a place
Out of the way
Where they could be kept
Stored or forgotten
I tried my head
But my brain complained of conditions cramped
I tried my lungs
But as they filled with sharp thought it was hard to breathe
Surely my liver would help
But it claimed the contents too toxic
Looking around I found
My unsuspecting heart
Small and smooth
With chambers practical and hidden
As I fed the feelings in
They disappeared beneath muscle memory
The pump continued to hum
Relieved, I turned
Dusted my hands and walked away
Only later to learn, dismayed
That the heart doesn't hide
It condenses

Ursa Major

I search for a place to conceal love
In the barefoot evening grass
The aroma of fresh sawn cedar
With solemn calls of a distant train
Perhaps a slice of devil's food cake

I settle with the evening sky
When no sees me
I stretch up with my eyes
Trace the handle, smile
And stir up a vision
As I fill inside

Choosing Paths

Untenable situations
Stuck between putting an end to what never was
And letting it wash
Can one grieve something that never existed?
Can one hold and let go?
Nothing is ever captured
Or owned
Grips are fragile at best
Take time to cradle love for a little while
As everything known deteriorates
A slow march
Left to wonder
Eternally crestfallen

Memory of Thoughts

My firefly ideas light up, then go
Hummingbirds that flit and speed past
Squalls bring confusion and turbulence
Only a phantom of clouds remain

I wish they would last, stay longer
But just as the sandhills head south
My reverb escapes, imitates their rattle
Each day's change holds a prospect of growth

Sparkle and glow draw attention and awe
But the slightest of breezes unveil
A phoenix of a thought can leave an imprint
Ashes can be beautiful too

Paths to Spring

Mediation While Doing Chores: A Heart is a Heart, A Leaf is a Leaf

after William Carlos Williams–*A Golden Shovel*

You already know that trees breathe. So
why are you surprised they talk and that much

of what they say goes unheard? It depends
on how well you listen. Root upon

root, the mycorrhizal connections are like a
hand in a hand. White pine, yellow birch, red

cedar, black locust — regardless the color wheel
of pulp or skin, they connect beneath the barrow,

conferring in the same dirt. As a grove goes sick, glazed
by disease or the stress of our heat, so can we. See with

your heart, not your eyes, that shine or rain
we all deserve to exist — every furry creature, or water

bound bug, or vines that twine, or you and me beside
the beautiful horrors of living. It comes to mind as the

morning breeze helps the trees speak again, and white
beams peek through to illuminate feed for the chickens.

Flowers

for George Floyd

Locust petals fall,
summer snow pushed by change.
Winds shift,
blue sky turns gray
as windows streak with rain.
In my office, away from storms;
                                        virus and protest—
I bear witness.
White blossoms and dark branches
combine to make life
possible.

Cicada

Jovial in the backyard,
earthen and soiled,
my children asked
the source of the buzzing.

Listening past the neighbor's mower
I hear the monotonous call.
In dim jubilation,
the cicadas are awake.
Their energy brims,
cycling through song, alive
in the dreadful heat of summer,
singing as if winter doesn't exist.
Anxious to put the dark times behind,
vaguely aware of their fate.

The sun sets past our porch
while man's exoskeleton,
the interstate highway,
whines just beyond sight.
I consider my commitments and responsibilities,
and how my kids have been taught
to thankfully accept the same fate.
Some days music is all that soothes.
Perhaps the best thing to do
is return to the ground
instead of drowning in droning sound.
Our shells are all that's left,
eventually one with the loam.

Monarch

By way of kings and queens
A yearning so deep
That it survives death
3 generations removed
Yet it knows
Beckoned to fly
Memory in the cells
Smart velvet sails
With an invisible compass
That tells it where to find nourishment
Rest and refuge
Before riding vectors south
It passes revenants of parents,
                                        grandparents,
                                                    greats.

Once left as an egg
Rich in its center
No eyes, no heart
Having never been home
Life's baton
On the milkweed's underside
That became the caterpillar
Which spun its shell
To chrysalize inside
Purpose and beauty eclose
With wings wet
To dry and ride streams

It takes to the sky to continue
To pass and live again

As it searches for Yucatan
It mystically knows
That oyamel grove
Miles above the sea
Like some innate map

I'll find my way
A winterbourne spirit
Only to turn around
Leaving clues and history
An infinite inception

Connections

I sent you a message
that went unanswered
and I stewed.

But I realize
that friendship is no different
than sandbars on the river,
aging goats prairies,
the patterns of clouds,
or a seasoned fencepost.
Everything is itself
only once.
As days pass
time alters the strands that connect us.
There is no inherent good or bad in this
but it happens whether we want it or not.

When a child's hand destroys a spider web,
the spider builds a new web
with different points of contact.

Maple

I am the silver in the yard
Homestead pillar
Steadfast and stoic
I provide fireworks in the Autumn
Protection from the wind
A place to climb and hide from the world
As reminders gently copter down to the grass
They rest beside new brackets at my base
My broad shoulders spread wide
Leaves blot out the sun
Shade creator
My family's content with me

But soon a storm will come
From horizons unseen
To bluster and blow
At my heart rot hidden
Behind branch and bark
You'll never know
Until the crack snaps
Now all are wide—eyed
Staring at the hole inside
How vulnerable I was
How exposed

Looking for Morels

From asphalt to gravel
Gravel to grass
A passage from meadow to hinterland
Where the anemone and trillium
Mimic half—melted snow
Winter's grip easing
                                        not quite let go
Scan the canopy for the skeletons
Of smooth standing elms
In a state of undress

                                        I search for life in death
Delicate mushrooms
Camouflaged in decay
The shy ones hide in plain sight
How many missed, I'll never know

A fresh picked handful
Swings in an old onion sack
                                        Delivered
To my cousin with cancer
I find can no longer eat
As she camouflages decay
Her unconsumed gifts
She gives them away

Thrush

You say you're happy with who you are
Where you're at
But it's also like you're a wood thrush
In the midst of the deepest, dimmest forest
Singing your little heart out
Hoping someone will appreciate you
Pining to be heard by someone who cares
Someone that listens to you and asks for more
I come to you because I hear your song
Striking and strong among the moss and phloem
Each exhale a lush present for the world
The darkness lifts a little when your melody carries
Through the bark
Past the cambium
Straight into the memory of my heartwood
Find yourself in that timber
Build a nest
Sleep in the serenade of your soul

Sheridan Lake/Spring Creek

2004

The goosebumps could be from the cool
or from the energy in this canyon.
The water and rumble of rapids pull us closer.
On the banks of the creek
the sweet smell of pine
surrounds nature's pantry.
The boughs flex and wave.
With each crunch forward
I hear my needle footsteps.
I stop to absorb and breathe,
oddly at home amongst the rock and dust.
No Sauron cell towers,
no civil suits,
or high cholesterol traffic.
Just the comfort of a vinyl shell–
me, my father and ol' Maggie makes three.
We are limitless, like a prairie breeze.

2008

I reminded myself that shorter trips are still trips.
Morning came
accompanied by the promise of rainbow trout
and a cup of hot coffee.
The habits of breathing and breakfast
are all that stood between me
and the spillway.
A careful check of my tackle,
a test of the bike tires,
sandwich, granola and a Braeburn apple.

Hopped my bike, pushed pedals,
decamped seeking limits.
I'll drift lines as my children sleep.

2012

Time blasted past
and the greying dog
plodded into the wetness,
lapped between pants
and drank deep.
My dad had less hair and more patience.
I attempt to seamlessly pass a baton
like I am my own season.
As the day turned to night
I watched, heard the lake
massage the shore,
as my son sat,
tucked tight in my lap.
Our eyes glowed
a brilliant warm orange,
camouflaged from the cooling air
by a skin of fleece.
We sensed evening's approach
as it nipped at our necks
and the Jack Pine flames fought it off.
I sensed life elapsing
and imagined
I would fight my way
back to these memories
for the rest of my days.
That time, that place,
beside the stream, the lake,

where we collected
our souls and the expiring sun.
We discovered then
what I know now:
the witching hour
is for everyone.

To Quell a Drought

Of what flows away
Much will come back
So open
Let it run

Give to receive
Love and be loved
Let your breath be the breeze
Be kind and the world smiles

Water evaporates
Clouds form
When the rain falls
Water pools again

Drifting Seams

There's a certain eddy to this current
That I've yet figured out
It bows and curls
To unforeseen stops
Then riffles in a rush
Over rock and old trunks
I seek to discover how to float with devoir
Without getting hung up or twisted in knots
Give just enough slack
To reach the pockets and bunkers
Tucked beneath the bank
Midway between bottom and surface
When I relax and allow a natural presentation
I'll have a chance to lure the brilliance within

Triptych: Heaven and Earth

what if
I don't dive but
rise
caught in a thermal
not of my making
light in my love
present to the heavens

when I fall
I float away
like a feather
destined for a nest
bonded with mud
repurposed—I hatch
new life

from my body
transformed I
flurry, twist
divine
and stick
feet on the ground
I ascend

Proven

for Ben Ahlstrom

I can see you in the dark hours,
hunched over the wheel,
breath in the air.
Knowing where you've been,
not sure where you're going,
unable to stop.
What did you think
when you hit the barricade?
In the dead of night?
In -35°?
While the winds reshaped the landscape?
Your tracks were covered as you made them.
Bedded down in the snow
like you floated to your rest
in the peace of cold.

Sweet Nothings

In times of unrest
we cry out.
Mother puts the pines to her lips
and calms us,
stirs with a turn of the earth.
Find comfort in her voice,
peace in her touch.

Rebirth

I rest beside a pile of split oak,
and notice a murder of crows.
The world's breath stops
to listen to the raucous cussing.
Calls and echoes report,
suddenly scatter,
break their black pattern
when I grab my maul.
Corvus cackle in tongues
and know things I don't know.
Today their voices were clear,
telling all that will listen:
before winter comes autumn,
and a deathly frost
is the only true path to spring.

Restoration

for Hayden

I drive my heel to the spade,
the spade to the earth.
I rake the humus and rock.
The warm, soft pulp of life
and the cold, hard suspended realities.
I gently untangle your roots,
carefully tuck you in.
Both of us are comforted.
If I can keep the weeds at bay
and the rodents away,
my sapling might have a chance.
Carry on and do what I cannot.
Bound the earth and life as one.
To shade and shelter
thoughts and ideas,
resist the fires,
and stand as a monument
to the way things can be.

Star Charts

Space Between

Property, belongings, they are a pleasure to own
Well, some things, at least
Useful tools, for example
Suitable clothes
A gold ring
Some change to jingle and sing in a pocket
In the end, these are still only things
We place the significance on them
Placards of our privilege
Sometimes like we swaddle a baby
Sometimes like we swat a fly
Sometimes like a bible
They can be broken
Lost or stolen
But the memories generated
Are more precious

Magic resides in the immaterial;
                                                            the kerning of life
Not the spatula, rather
The smell of cinnamon wafting from the kitchen

The way the seasons change
The sound of wood curling beneath plane
The sweetness of wild columbine
The soft page of a billet—doux
The persistence of a stream
The saltiness of mouthbound tears
The presence of an evening loon
The squeeze of amorous words

The steady growth of a hickory
The coo of a little one
The tone of speaking leaves
The way two hands can fit together
Everything mystic interlocks
An expanding accretion of meaning
Crossing in a pageant of oneness

Galaxy

When I look up on a clear night
I see the perfect pinpricks
And the soft brush of cream
I let the universe control my breath
Transparent across the sky
I marvel and feel little
Lost in cosmic spaces

It's like being in her orbit
Spread wide, slow pull to center
Glow giving spirit
Each star brings something different
Aligned in her sky
Heavenly bodies
Held by her gravity

Boundary Waters

I slip through and glide
You softly speak as I touch
I'm glad your clarity allows me to gaze
At your structure below
For I have traveled long and far
Just to see the heavens reflected in your deep pools
Let your fragrance sweep through me
At the end of these 6 days
I will portage no more
Except to travel back
To you in my sleep

Story of the Rising Sun

Ballad for a Moonsick Maiden

There once was a lass who fell for the sun
In love with the light every time it would come
She welcomed the dawn more than anyone
Cloudy days upset her

The sun smiled back at this curious face
Spreading light other places seemed such a waste
The sun always felt it was in the right place
Until it met this young woman

Early one eve the girl started to cry
The sun went to leave and the girl whispered "why?"
The sun gave her a gift as a friendly reply
And the moon made its appearance

The girl filled with delight and committed her soul
By the light of the moon she'd live her life full
To see night and day gave her total control
Except for when she was sleeping

Though she noticed the moonlight shortened each day
She begged for the moon to linger or stay
In the daytime she'd breathe and at night she would pray
Because she couldn't handle the dark

Then one tragic eve the moon didn't call
When she sought out its light the girl took a fall
She fell into a river, and like a rag doll
She settled right on the bottom

When the day came around with exuberant grace
The sun looked for the girl all over the place
It eventually went down with a frown on its face
Pledging to look more tomorrow

So up to this day the fireball looks
Searches high, searches low, while the earth slowly cooks
Its determination is one for the books
And that's why it always comes up
        Daily it never gives up
        Seeking smiles to fill it back up
        And keep it from going away

Miss

I pull alongside where the river slacks
Water flat and wide
Sable tones of earth this night, contrast
The moon renders the surface silver
Backwater dotted with pads and dens
Effervescent sheen of lifeblood
Slight shadow tracing green and grey
Crickets and whistles cast at a distance
I breathe deep —close my lids
Across the bluffs and moraine, I roll
My third eye open wide
To same light on skin
Curves and lips move tranquil within
Serpentine gaze locked

There's no escape from everywhere
She's set in mind, fathoms
Her body
Her soul

Radiance

When the pitch sticks
And all is opaque
Remember, there's no place on earth
Where it's dark all the time

After the sun has set
It will rise again
Maybe blocked or obscured
But know that it's there

The poles?
For long periods, black
But they eventually brighten
Then stay alight

Even a place like Chicago
Where the fog shrouds our thoughts
Day and night exist
And the light changes with the seasons

The Sun to the Glacier

I scan the globe
For your majesty and prominence
You fill the valleys, reshaping granite
When you slowly push on
Your presence, unavoidable

I try to get close
Just to watch you recede
Shying from my warmth
Leaving bare the display
A litter of boulders and gray

I wish you back, cold beauty
To admire from a distance
Because the ground is a void
The flora is forgotten
Only lichens and what's left of you

Midwinter Meditation

To clear my mind in the middle of the solstice
I lace my boots,
stretch and tighten the strings –
brace for the cold air
and set down the road.
A north breeze keeps
the nearby interstate quiet.
It emphasizes the silence.
I feel the chill, tug
my hat fully over my ears,
pull my gloves tighter,
and wear my anxiety, or
the day's conflicts.
Once outside I try to bury it all.
Revert to simplicity.
A carpet of stars overhead.
If not for the lack of light
I would see my own breath.

Just as so many slumber,
close their eyes
to the world, I walk alone.
Yet my sleeping brethren and I
turn together into the night,
spinning on a planet
always halfway drenched in darkness.
Amniotic space surrounding us
like we are still waiting for our birth.
Faint glows, strong pitches, low hums.
I possess a strange connection to the emptiness.

I look up to spy the Ursas, major —minor;
I know there is nothing between us but space.
Me and Polaris.
If I had an eternity, I would walk to her
curl my body and nuzzle her bosom,
and apologize, as a good Midwesterner would do.
For her, I'll do anything.
I will give my heart to others,
I will promise to do better,
and I will bask a moment in her radiance
before walking home.

20 minutes later
I am back in the living room
removing my boots,
returning to tea,
preparing for sleep.

My thoughts revolve with the world,
away from my past,
through the black.
Eventually all becomes bright again.
When tomorrow arrives
we can be born once more,
each day
a chance to be new.

Constellations

From where I look now
Our celestial bodies
Are divided by vastness
Strangers passing by
Look up and glimmer
Light years away

With a change in perspective
We could be binary stars
Colors combined
And use each other's brilliance to shine brighter
Build somatic energy
Fight the emptiness — together

Hunting

I watch my son sit on fallen oak leaves
while he rests in the arms of a deadfall.
The breeze is a slow breath.
His head next to a carpet of moss spores,
he sleeps.
The sun shines through thinning canopy,
catching spider lines in the light–
twinkle their daytime constellations.
Nuthatches cry while crickets play their dirge.
By comfort or exhaustion,
he sheds his anxiety for contentment.
Even amid death
all is right with the world.

Grounded

Not the requisite stars
   or flowers
Not the mist
   or seductive glances
I will romanticize
   the decay
The consumption
   and compost
That the trees and grasses
   sprout from
For the holiest places
   are where we plant our feet
Heaven always lies
   beneath us

On the Way Home

I drove down a road with no comers or goers.
Pavement empty.
Cloud deck low – the speakers high.
Sounds of my youth crooned
and filled the car
to the point I could feel the guitars.
When halfway home,
in the midst of Soma,
all by myself,
I felt my breath shorten.
The normalcy of errands and domestic life
had been listening too, and they were scared.
The song had reached
into my deepest recessions,
past my thin skin and flesh to my bony core,
to pluck from me the seed of my peachy existence.
A small thing, a pittance,
but declaring uranium's weight.
It was held in front of me,
shining and wet.
It's from these that melancholy grows.
The dense thimble of sadness extracted,
plumb with anxiety. I thought
I had placed all that safely out of mind.
Yet that which was hidden was before me.
It *was* me,
beating and throbbing.
The wellspring opened to
the march of memories, heartache and loneliness.
They flooded my thoughts

and spilled out my eyes.
As I pulled in the driveway
I beat it all back
into its crevasse,
wondering exactly what had happened.
Dumbfounded and confused,
it dawned
that the apprentice knew not
the power of the stars and song
until he unknowingly put them together.

Aurora

A door opened tonight
where it was too high to fly
so I climbed my mind's ladder
to be near you

Nestled in blue
at peace with the world
I moved close to your satin
soaked by rapture

Trimmed in red
splashing green
slow shimmering
your light moves prove elusive

Left my vessel behind
now I'm somewhere between
the life I live and
my eternal

Amen

A lone night light flickers
in a child's room after
a chapter from a Star Wars book.

Dad, how far is space?

What do you mean?

How far does space go?

That's a great question, buddy.
I don't know.

Who does?

I'm not sure
that anyone knows.
'Cause it flows where we can't see.
Scientists, teachers and wise
wise men
aren't sure
for lack of proof —
some people think
it goes on for infinity.

What's that?

Infinity means forever.
So space would go on
and on
and never stop.

(silence)

I hope I can take
a rocket into space some day.

You do?

Yeah, you know why?

No, why?

I think space goes all the way
into the bible,
so if I blast into space
and keep going,
I can fly into the bible.

(silence)

Their spirits drift,
the wall clock ticks
in the darkening room
with only one light.

Experiential Cartography

Amid a Storm in Pleasant Hill Township

Standing on the gravel ridgetop road
Lightning flashes and thunder cracks close
Close enough to pierce my eyes
Bright vine grows quick, then gone
A ghost of the fissure in my vision
My ears hit with a shrill tone
Bloom of ozone sweet on the nose
The reverberation moves through me
A rumble and shake in my chest
It casts down into the valleys
Rolls farther down still
Seeps past the trees and underbrush
Unfurling fast and slow
The rumble echoes and breathes and
Lives a long moment before it dies
A steady diminish
The light existed for only a moment
Yet was part of me
As I stand among fat drops
And pitter—pats
Wet to the point of not caring
I wonder exactly where I'd be
If I flashed and exploded
And pushed myself outward
Dissipating to nothing
So that I may live
Just once
Inside another

Deconstruction on MN Hwy 43

A fox lived at the turn of the highway,
past the quarry north of Rushford.
Its house was a small burrow
fixed within rock.

I watched it follow the roadside,
a steady trot, determined steps,
on its way elsewhere,
with hopes to return.

The raid of a giant henhouse
is a remnant of a past
that is no longer in existence,
alongside the farmer's concern

of its teeth. My music blares
as I give a wide berth,
making my way with Coltrane
and his spinning reeds.

The days mixed
and my path brought me
through weeks later. I saw her,

mama fox with two kits
trailing behind. I delighted
watching her show them

the way. She
like so many moms: the one

at the supermarket who wiped

the trail of snot
from her toddlers nose, the one
who led hers through the crowded church

parking lot, the one
that visited the food shelf
to bring back vittles for dinner,

even my wife who once helped
our pups choose their own clothes.
Like my own mother, who I'd see soon.

Later
that summer,
coming down
off the same ridge, I search
for free jazz, switching
the station away
from more news of murder.

Ukraine under siege.
Gaza pounded to oblivion for refusing to give Israel back
its daughters and sons.
The ever—present hunger in The Horn.

—I traveled past
the known spot
to see the mother
fox standing over a fresh dead
cub on the shoulder,

a statue in the sun
waiting for her little one to rise.

Her orange—red fur

makes me break,

a warning, knowing

the company she keeps.

I divert my eyes and speed

past, her body hunched

in the rearview.

On the Back Porch at Whit's End

High above a holler filled with fields and fruit
Next to bold oaks and acorn rain

A cloudbank rests around me
I cannot see what I picture is there

That the farmer started his chores
Signaled by bellered notes in the blindness

Dark flashes must be flycatchers
Delivering food to newly hatched life

Nature conceals itself
Behind a damp curtain

I feel like the fog sometimes
More imagination than reality obscured

Without true sight, I search inside
And look closer, past neurons

I wonder if nothing is ever whole
Ever touches

Or if life's pockets vibrate in unison
Drawn on the strings that move between all

In the empty tin can of the universe
Echoes are deep and unending

Just like the sun coming ‘round
To give warmth to the soil

I look toward my feet, grounded, as the mist moves
Towards the end it lifts and draws in spirals

Whisps retreat and reveal the green valley
Just in time to see a fox scamper through pasture

Out of the corn and over terraced cow paths
With a fresh meal fast in his mouth

As the pieces continue to dissipate
I finally see the barn, the grass,

Guernseys meander uphill
Droplets carry on with their skyward climb

As the vapors give way
I see the land as I did yesterday

I’m still a small man on big hill
Where things are starting to come into view

Moonshine Gulch Saloon

Somewhere there's a crease in the earth that asks
where you headed?
And you try to remember why, or even where
you are, exactly.
You begin to think like the surface of a bubble,
taut and elastic,

forming at the top of a cold bottle, towards
the end of dust and a long day. The spit on your lips
comes with an answer that flicks you further

than you've been in your shallow life. Maybe you'll need all those
unswizzled sticks as you condemn laws and god's damnation,
bringing to the fire your desire for companionship and connection.

Except you didn't prognosticate the follow up *where you going?*
Your tracks stop in the buzzing air, and it will drizzle rain
in the days to come. You laugh and drink, airborne beers clink,

and you eat burgers and fried brown stuff, and you realize
you're only headed as far as your eyes can see. Paths that will
send you 'round next Black Hills bend, to the next gulch.

Gulch after gulch, you navigate your way because
you know there are brews in chilled glasses and unplanned
potato salad and celebration among exasperation and

friendly peoples and lazy dogs on porches and maybe
some fireworks and it doesn't matter how many moose
are on the walls or who is in office or whose round of
drinks

this is or how many trout are in the streams...
because it only matters that you crack a longneck
with strangers and form new clans, and breathe it in

and sip, and breathe it in. Nestled in a quick glance from
a stolen moment, you watch the deer on the opposite side
of the road find ancient crossings and feel what
contentment

might be. 5 minutes, or days, or years from now,
as the mulies come
off the steep banks, eternal, seemingly without wit,
they cross the road
like they've done it a million times before.

Past the Vermillion Cliffs

I often wonder if the Universe
looks down upon us, upon
earth, you and me,

and sees the lights aligned
and notices any similarities.
If, like me, it ponders dark spaces

between. Maybe it marvels
up there at the concentration of lights
it sees near masses of water below.

Maybe, like me, it dreams of walking
in daylight, to roam free
from sea to rivers to sea.

Maybe it's a witness to the chaos
and distress in the congregation.
On land at night, I bet we look like

just another galaxy, pulsar unstable
in the center. Maybe it
ignores us and goes about

its dark life, working for
something, who knows what,
a cheap thrill, a new comet, a beer,

a certain collision with another
swirling sphere. Or not.
Because when I look up

and see the swaying clouded
cluster of stars in their hazy
stripe through our sky,

I wonder what rivers and lakes
lie inside it, near those amalgamations,
where there is business

and commerce and disconnection.
I reflect on what it would be
like, awash in the bright

waters, large arcs
of branches flowing nearby, past
stars that connect the celestial.

I bet I can feel alone
in that density too.
A solitary body among others,

at any age, in any language,
occulted from view.
Like the boy I saw. After a day

of driving through open space
and sand in a world colored
by the past, I stopped for air

and water at a convenience store,
a gas station, a modern museum
full of ice and more things

I didn't have to have.
Inside, the racks displayed packages
wrapped in shiny cellophane.
Isles of air fresheners, quarts of
synthetic oil, candies, nuts,
sparkling water and soda encased

with the Corona. Like the heavenly bodies
I spy, everything dense, stacked
so I see dull glints and outlines,

none of it wanted in the moment.
The boy came in with his family
as I stood at the back by the

cooler. Mother and father
arguing in Italian, bored older sister
with buds in her ears, and him

sporting black shorts and Dunks.
Their commotion disturbed
the Arizona dust. He came to the

counter clutching a yellow bag of Starburst
for the road, a little something
to pass his time. With a wry slide

his bright treats are pressed closer
to the register, rung after he's told
to put them back. No one else paid

attention. His black curls, his olive skin
pin light in his eyes, and a soft
horizontal line on his shirt.

He turned and briefly looked
back at me with invisible needs
and desires. That boy was the

universe. I think of him tonight,
on the deserted streets of Fredonia,
where I'm just one person searching

under a streetlamp,
watching the sun's rays recede,
casting wishes upon the headlights

that streak over the road,
quasars that cruise into the center
of darkness. I know it's the same

light the Milky Way sees, because
when I close my eyes and hear it speak
through the thin, arid night,

I hear a wish to simply be seen.

Off-Roading to Papakōlea While Contemplating a Poet Who Told Me to Steal

Far from any bar,
too close to the Pacific,
my beard a half—drift of honey and thorns.
The dust tells me
don't look for treasure
where there isn't any, or reason where there is none.
My head,
an empty chest that might make a good drum.
Day trip, driven
to a beach
where I may not return. I see
others work harder. I'm told
the labor in getting there
is worth it.
The truck hovers a moment, then lurches,
a microcosm of my beating pulse,
the wheels
undulate beneath jolted shocks,
the rubber circles
turn and catch volcanic earth, grass—
cast pebbles and dirt.
The tires stop
before the torque explodes
to the next fulcrum
as we crawl forward
toward the green sand,
microscopic peridot that paints the basalt.
In the fray

my hand lands on her thigh
when I nearly fall, then
slips up her skin to her leg's lips
with the next toss,
fingers grazing her bikini bottoms.
She whispered
honey! like
a borrowed breath, a plea,
a half-processed sugar
stuck in her mouth—
it reminds me of the time I heard a poet
read the word
"honey" at least
3 times like it was nothing,
like a conjuring,
like it made all his words stickysweet when he boasted
a clean thief's confession,
legs full of borrowed pollen, his performance
a vampire's reflection,
while the audience
pawed the floor like a bull in the idol's ballroom,
gleaming eyes prepared to dance,
plump moon on the sea
excited by this strange sorcery,
the night's air made weird, crusty, full.
I see now how he had the courage
to fight tomorrow with his bareknuckled fists.
I hold that moment,
the bard's reading, like a doubloon.
Now it is mine to keep. My gold.
The truck's cab shudders me back,
and in this way

it goes, as I travel over the raw,
carved terrain until the vehicle reaches a softer path
and all smoooooths out.
The waves are alive
and the wind stings us with sand.
The verdant shore grows
mythic in my mind. All the colors
of all the beaches, a prism of complexion.
I breathe.
Are there more grains
made from pulverized rock and quartz,
pummeled and polished,
at our feet and beneath the surf,
or more snowflakes on earth?
How far
does that pendulum swing,
widening a gap
in the shifting balance?
In the sun blasted sand with the glimmer of stars
the waves toss us tired
and we leave the beach
satiated, but our hungers
will write their own stories.
We navigate the maze home,
sunglasses sprayed by the sea,
damp bikini's and suits,
gemstone filled creases,
and minds chocked with wonder
and lust. Later, when the sun sinks,
the bulged end of a wooden wand
in honey, I wash my beard wholly.
This day, like each before is stolen; complete.

To the Woman at the Front Desk of the Americas Best Value Inn & Suites

It's too early for cheery remarks
But you've been up for hours
Started your shift at 4, you said
Made the coffee
Assembled breakfast
Apologized for things not your fault
And likely put up with the worst of us
As we settle up, my daughter and I quibble
About how to best split 20 hours in the car
8 and 12
13 and 7
11 and 9
You join with a grin
Suggesting new numbers —new math
I am not in the mood
Another grumpy traveler
But in that moment, I stop
And I watch
And I listen
And I saw you
Haggard yet chipper
You with your thin hair pulled back tight
You with your band—aids and bruises
You with your cheaters hanging around your neck
With your tattoos, names
And other numbers
                    Life and death displayed
Of what might be your journey
Cigarettes at your side

That emerge from your purse
Whose leather is beaten, cracked
Faded and tired
Maybe the smokes help
To get you through your 10-hour shift
Your second in as many days, you said

These words contain my ignorance
And my gratitude
For the coffee whose grounds are not your fault
For the turbulence I imagine you've had
For you and what you bring
For your smirk amid the desolation
For your perseverance
Thank you, I say
For our receipt
Born of opportunity
When my daughter asks
I bet she doesn't get paid much
Probably not
Why is she so happy?
I survey the price of gas
Ascending over the summer
Across the highway and down the street
To a hawk that leaves a litter filled ditch with its kill
Money's not the only thing

The young hand pauses on the handle
To imbed in memory
As we get in the car
Head west
Head north
Across the ink
And the scars
Of America

Sauntering Thoughts from a St. Paul Hotel Window

It's summer and I'm waiting for the Juncos to come back. They always do. Their tracks in the snow are pictographs in my dreams. Like the voices I admire, I will scribble things I can't translate. Perhaps worthy of reading someday, or at least given a cursory view, past graveyards and trees and boxcars. And words will become the fur of a horse brushed clean, whisps of rabbit cooked vapor after a storm, creaking under thunderous steps on a wood floor. I will see poems in your squint when the sun lights your skin, I will see them in the paint pushed off your toes by aging nails, I will see them in the busy insects and the birds and the sky, I will feel them in the space where five days ago and five months ago and five years ago share a sameness, and I will gather untamed letters and fold them neatly to save them for later. I will give them back to those I pass, and I will proselytize the strange and good in churches of my own making, places where I am not ashamed to be both broken and whole, be a congregation of myself, where sermons will be understood as much as one can understand, and there is an eternal potluck, for I will always bring what I need to sustain, like how trees drink, like how a fish breathes, how any sentient creature can love. I'll follow this poem as it takes the elevator down into the dingy lounge, out the security doors, through the greasy streets, by gutters and grasses, over the bridges, to a wilderness only defined by fear and comfort and serenity, side-by-side-by-side.

Kintyre

(46.5501° N, 99.9492° W)

I. The Roads
Over the glacier scraped soils
Lies a network of dark lines
To spirit trains or semis
Commodities sent to people and places
In return for empty containers
The highways move from concrete to asphalt
Eventually to gravel and dirt
Places where names are spoken, not marked
Years known by their yields
Neighbors measured in miles
Paths narrow with turns
To leagues of run-down farmhouses
They keep the unused barns company
They once hosted families
Now rented to hunters of fowl
Grasses grow between the paver cracks
Paint peels, floors creak
Prairie air on all sides
Plastic surrounds the windows
Half the light switches stuck in place
By cracked and yellowed tape
Full of cold, drafty spots
These homes are ghosts of themselves
Abandoned years ago
Farmers took their lives
Down the driveways
To a new ones down the road

II. A Farmhouse
Some evenings the sun
is a match on the plains,
burring through clouds
and blazing the fields.

It's just another fire to survive.
Which I do when I arrive
and clear the gear
from my truck bed.

I set decoys sit in the dust
of an unlocked garage,
next to the unlocked house,
near a tractor with the keys in it.

Provisions brought inside and unpacked
then embraces are exchanged with the party.
We eventually settle in a place of importance.
There is gravity in a farmer's kitchen.

A place where history and decisions
were made from a church cookbooks.
We exist between the modern and primal,
where the knob on the crock pot works if wiggled.

I think about an unowned past,
to a place where rakers of the land ate.
Ancestors came by foot or hoof or wagon or train.
Left their sod houses for timber and brick.

I think of the certain hells they suffered.
Bouts of starvation or dysentery,
the sweltering heat of summer,
somehow surviving the frozen blows of winter

with little more than kerosene and candles.
A bible and rifle their only protection.
They carved out their living
as the natives did before them,

communing, alone on the plains.
Like the single utensil left out:
a well-worn spoon on the stove,
wooden and stained from its past.

My mind wanders as I search empty drawers
beneath the piles of dead flies in the sink.
Outside the feral cats wait, bellies soon full
from the offal of our bounty.

The faucet whines when I turn it on.
The water runs until it clears, liquid
piped from The Big Muddy
miles and miles away.

I stand on the faded linoleum,
worn by hardy bootsoles of the past,
thankful for what's changed and what hasn't.
The old man on the wall still with grace like he found

a way to escape the pastoral prints
that line the dining room walls.

The clock ticks slow, battery low,
while I study the school project string art.

A web of carefully wound wool
threaded with steady young hands,
framed and placed by the phone,
the image of a buck and his rack.

It's a skill we can learn and reminds me
how everything is taught—
flora and fauna and the cruel humankind
residing on one thread together.

III. A Rented Room

Fortune is a father who's a friend. For me, fortune abounds. After dinner we play cribbage and drink. The fading light makes bourbon a shade darker. There are skunks and runs and bump after bump before we gather our waders and ammo. Fortune favors the prepared. For now, fortune abounds. We gather 'round and swap stories, make plans, and say stupid shit, talking smart. My dad spreads the wrinkled maps on the table where boundaries are observed and noted, and we won't talk about shortcomings or spats. Potential flyways traced with the tip of a finger sliding on paper to a slough that looks like my heart. We drum up the past, the years the birds beat us, and remove our hats when we bring up our loves and our flames. Our motors and minds are constant but decline as we run out of gas. We retreat to our bunks as we bid each other good night. The floor is silent now that we stopped. Our alarms ready, set near our beds as the intoxication of dream slows our breathing. We hear the whistle of wings through places foreign and familiar, in this house that is not of our making. We peel back our sheets and slide in, cover ourselves with clean blankets that we trust are free of pox and intention, and allow ourselves to slip and drift, give way to the sands as we become hourglass grains that bring great animals and peace. Making space for these moments is hard, but most good things worth doing are. Fortune is a green head in range while my dad calls the shots. For then, fortune abounds.

IV. Hunting Over Water

Predawn morning rituals
Visions of the day to come
A dark drive
A darker setup
Until the rose hip aurora
Splashes duckweed and bulrush
Methane of mire swirls
Decoys and blinds set
Whitetail sheds in the muck
Ring-necks cackle and thrum
Nimble coon search the stubble
A shotgun blaze signals dawn
And the canvasbacks head for deep lakes
Dogs bark at new shapes
As we're concealed in camo
Forgetting is slow and pleasant
Absent the urgent mail and demands
A day's tab already paid
The torture of network news, nonexistent
When a gust picks up and encircles
Any transgressions can travel
The windswept sloughs
Spilled coffee, spilled blood
All in the past
Nothing promised except maybe the next minute

To sit and wait for the bluebills
Where the reeds bend in the breeze
And the cottonwoods float
Aimless, fresh casualties
Seeds that break the surface
Of these North Dakota days

V. Leaving The Land

At the end of my time in North Dakota I head back to the present, down from the town that is short of the slope, past the Red River and the drift of prairie circulating from the heart of the coteau.

Road signs on the highway follow the fields I pass, graveyards of ranches and skeletons of corroded tractors.

Blackbirds and pheasants call near fence lines as I cross over.

I know the Missouri has run from brown to white and the endless sky spills light for miles on the ascent and fall of crops, grass and rock.

The season is passing from green to rust and the land looks fallow and starved.

Wheels turn and another evening settles around me, where the silhouettes of ducks on the water are just reverse constellations.

I drive by new windmills that flash red dots in the pitch, where the blades whisper a bison's breath and the names flash by like the days have gone —Mandan, Sioux, Gross, Svanes, Weigel, Johnson–

Perhaps the encroaching night signals that the hills are
begging to be charred and reset by a torch never passed.
Perhaps the plains must burn before they are fertile again.

I can light my torch with these words.
Regardless of inhabitants the earth is eager to show it
doesn't give a damn about time, or ownership, you, me,
graveyards or trees.

No matter how much we want it to the ground we stand
on never cared.
Never will.

Camping in My Parent's Yard on the 4th of July

for Andi

In the night
A shower passed
The water still drips
As another day lapses
Stacatto sounds
From canopy crowns
A downpour long gone
Ghost notes on nylon
Memories and kisses
From those who've moved on

O'Leary Lake

I break from the trail and catch a glimpse of the water
I see the glimmer through an archway of treetops
I know this is it
It's like the first snow that pulls me close to the window
Or the light green sepals of a pregnant orchid
A gravity holds tight
And I will stand motionless
Hand on a knob
Consumed by a hidden sign
That says "Enter"

How I got here does not matter
But the recognition of arrival
Slides into the keyhole
It unlocks the water and sun
Air and the lightness of being
Internal blaze is reeled in with the fireline
I put down my rod with my tension and desires
I can feel my attachment to the granite
The boulder on the shore
Which has occupied that space
Since before I was born
I have been but a cog on most days
Budgeted, spent
Encumbered, owned
What's left in me is pulled over the lake
A hidden current
A wild call
All breath

I chisel this place
Behind barriers of mind
So that I may go back
When a pall is cast
And the winds signal a gale
I come again to this sacred space
Ruminate — then repeat
Watch the water crest close to shore
Where resignation is no solution
Because it's May
And the pike are active again

Awakened in Beaver Creek Valley

Tidal conscience returns, concealing
the stones of a dream.

Sound seeps in
with our eyes drawn shut.
Pileated laughter
precedes dead wood knocking.
Thrush and finch babble
over distant turkey cutts.
Wings flit in dimness,
around and through thicket.
Sharp beaks hungry
for scarabs and grubs.

Our star
fishes through foliage,
casting down ridges.
As light hooks the
top of our tent,
eyelids float open, and
part the glowing blood.

Morning spawns,
as we rest in bed, sailing on
composted leaves.
Tent walls are damp
from our stale breath
and sag slightly inward.
Depressions are comfy.
Sleep longer, sleep

until the cardinal arrives to
chip-chip on branches
and sing as he flies:
Come, come –
the world is alive!

Waterways of the North

"Wilderness to the people of America is a spiritual necessity, an antidote to the pressure of modern life ..." Sigurd F. Olson, 1946.

Perhaps your path started like mine. A lifting dark where winding lines eventually widened. The water took me where I needed to go, not knowing if I was lost or if I soon would be, and this was alright. For deep inside the nest of losing is the place where findings drift and incubate. My path proceeded to a lake, an island. I was summoned by sounds, transfixed on a nameless radio voice sharing an excerpt from Sigurd Olson, an Earth Day commemoration, with orated chapters of *Reflections from the North Country*. That voice became a compass.

Perhaps you've been struck like I was. An awakening bolt. After the moment passed, like a storm come and gone, I scrambled for paper to scribble his name but got the first one wrong. It left me searching, fruitless months seeking his echo. His words haunted my bones, an undeniable resonation that whispered to me ... *you're part wild ... part free.*

Perhaps, like me, you've also been changed. A year after Olson's initial impact I was given cassette tapes, recordings of his writings in steady decline. I copied, looped, listened. And listened... conjuring forested dreams from a kindship with the words. I was raised in the Driftless bluffs, far from this mystical north, from Voyageurs, the BWCA, even Grand Marais. Places to escape today's chains and beastly demands. I made a plans with my dad to camp on Namakan, a week to visit and fish, and didn't realize part of me would stay.

in a tent drifting
thoughts are crumbs on campsite docks
that trip – my delta

II. Rainy River

Sigurd dreamt of The Bay,
Cedar in blood.
I was led to
Listening Point, to
Leopold, Snyder,
their dry wood kindles
in the boreal dusk.
from my shoal topsoil,
I will preach
to leave a better world

I envision the wilderness.
Loons occupy sleep.
new adventures, to
the Shack.
Jeffers, Berry–
a fire to connect
Shoots from my ash,
rise to witness the world.
and navigate my yearning
post arrival.

III. Rainy Lake

I was guided by spirits
on a pilgrimage to Mallard Island,
home of Oberholtzer's traces
and his selfless acts.
His refuge a triptych
of humanity, environment, and awareness.
On the selfish surface, my visit
appeased a need to absorb
legacy and vibrance, to infuse
the north in my soul.
In his drum room I opened
my bones down to the spine
as one would a good book.

So began creation through connection,
within myself, with humankind,
with the sensuous world.
As I went so can you.
Crack open brilliance,

expose the muse to light,
and seed dreams deep.
Thoughts are
just zygotes, waiting
to be born on the small
spit of rock, surrounded
by water that slowly lurches
towards the Churchill.

IV. Namakan Lake

The paddle slips through, and the water speaks, whispering tinges of songs that quietly quabble on the water's surface, leaving footprints in the wake.
In these places live silence in absence of man,
Absent of the rush and pace.
The wetness feeds the shore … it makes moist the earth and loam … it filters through moss and rock to the roots.

And I sit atop the wet.
It touches my vessel and touches me.
It quenches the world and quenches me.
It reaches through the Kevlar, into the boggy molecules and in and through bedrock, and the grass, and the soil, and everything clean.
I flow through it, and it flows through me.

The canoe's bow ploughs through waterways of old,
Where the Moose have gone … where the Cree have gone … where the Dakota have gone… where the Anishinaabe have gone… where the Voyageurs have gone … where the lumbermen have gone … where the adventurers go.

I have lost count of the portages, rods, but continue a steady beat.
And here is where I pick up in the rhythm of the woods,
Here I am present,
Here I am naked to God,
Here I am everything and nothing,
And here I am reborn by a glorious, righteous transformation.

In the dim dust of the trail the chickadees cut across my way.
The wild leeks peek up and the ferns sway as I pass.
I step with intention, careful of the stumpy twists of trees that attempt to trip me, and careful of my traces.
There is no contract, no shrine, and will never be.
The covenant is sealed inside me.

V. Namakan Narrows
We all need a center,
a place for return.
It can be heard where the crickets chirp,
caught in the flicker a husky bonfire,
or felt in the morning dew.
A place that is ours free and clear,
not through possession,
but through being —a wholeness.
Live right,
share and breathe.
The calls are for everyone.

VI. Little Vermillion Lake
Meet near the birdhouse
        Listen and see
Pistil and stamen
        Play games with pollen
Tree frogs purr
        Shallow runnels between
Surfaces pulled
        Wavelets pock and lap
White—throats whistle
        Back in the brush
Dancing at dawn
        Love-drunk dreamers
Kissed by the breeze
        Hear my breath
Hear me breathe
        Be one with this island
Beneath the pine trees

VII. Loon Lake
When the tremolo sounds
I am both here and gone

Where there is breeze and birds and sky
Where the water chats

Trees whisper and hush
To support the wailing trill

The loon sings uncommon into the night
A witness to the moon's bleeding

It wanes then fills, like a beating heart
As it slips past the rocks and the green

Tangerine to powder white
Ascend cloud and sky

The grayscale divers capture the rays
To reflect and burn in the black

Tearless eyes, laughter, cries
Heard from miles and miles away

When I close my lids I hear them still
Possess my waking days

VIII. Lac La Croix
Pour through pages
By authors long gone

Sometimes mountainous volumes by one man
Stand in an oxbow of words

Where thoughts once flowed freely
There is a stagnance of immortality

Exact thoughts
Don't go on forever

A cavalry of mold and armies of time
Battle integrity

With reinforced spines
There is strength to stand

A chance to be devoured
By the willing and hungry

So let us write for our own sakes
Slay our beasts

Or set them free
Conquer pages for the kingdoms

Our kingdoms
Where we are subject, jester, and royalty

IX. Saganaga Lake
I listened and read
When the dead man said
Play with abandon and zeal
Yet I lie here at night, afraid
        Of falling short
        Of the lake water's recession
        Of the toll modern life takes
        Of bears
        Of fulfillments not met
        Of the things I can see
and the hidden

        When what I must do is love

The flake of Norway Pine bark
The escape of the grid's grip
The water slapping and cupping shore
The smile of a child
The smell of rain
The lover breathing fast
The world known and obscured
Step outside to be inside
        Grounded to be free

X. Pidgeon River

The time is close for heavy hands and hearts to gather, close the cover, and carry on.

Paddle past sadness to bask in the glow of ever knowing that this,

this moment,

will always exist.

So, saunter in the dust.

Move sinew and muscle slow.

Permit a grace, an ease of living,

Always training for existence in the singing wilderness.

Whether moving or still, look to the water.

It will always glint in the daytime, as well as cloudless nights, by moon or starlight, evidence that whenever and wherever hope is present it can be recast.

So long as connections exists you cannot be a trophy, a trinket.

You may, however, become a lost memory, and this is alright.

Take on only what can be managed alone, and embrace experiences to deliver as stories.
Willfully gift to all that need.

XI. Lake Superior
On this strip of glaciated rock
the mull is young and light.

A weathered cedar stands against storms
to use what is given to survive.

Nightwalk on Tower Road

As the late June day cools
A call to stretch and wander stirs
My friend and I depart the house
We know some nights are blue like a flannel
A wave that wraps its limbs around us
To carry our thoughts through damp duff and moss
Suspended above the mantles of our chambers, our cores

We step to the twinkling that becomes more evident
A slip between shadows
Where a chill envelope of air brushes our skin
And reflective eyes shine in the distance
All that is shown of the creatures of the night
We see their light move but not their form
And agree we are among them

Our bodies and spirits
Move headlong into the night
On the lightness of the road that is faint against the dark
We trace the milky way with our eyes
Speak of the stars and constellations
And we try to think of what has been taught and forgotten
Our smallness and our absurdity
Beneath the night sky all is mystical
Awestruck by points of light that seem to charge our hearts

The road speaks under our feet
We walk near a set-aside field
Dead corn stalks stand in memory of the fields past
As the ground gets rest for later days

It will be primed and ripe for future crops
But its fruits this evening are of a different variety
In the field turned fey and wild
The illumination continues
As hundreds—perhaps thousands of fireflies
Flash and dance to circadian rhythms
Flying past our heads and outstretched arms
Playing games between cycles of light
Just as we do this night
In a space that is free of human politics
Free from knowing our scourge
As we escape the gravity of life's madness or the mundane
Through the confluence of points
Soon the sky and the field are one with specks
Our lives glow green blue and white

All the while, far to the east
Storms brew and flash on the horizon
Strobe low on the edge of the strata
Flow and pulse with energy
Strike the mind
We ponder what attracts us
What ignites

Continue down the gravel to the highway
Crossing the asphalt to a small country cemetery
Where many of the headstones are lit with small solar bulbs
Light-emitting diodes that seem to float
In remembrance of the stones owners
We flash our phones through the black at the granite
Read their names aloud in reverence with respect
Until the last one we pass displays the name *Bright*
And we fall silent in the moment
Commune with the stars
                    and the fireflies
                              and the lightning
                                        and the dead

Before we wordlessly move back across the blacktop
Meander through the dewy grass
Stare back at the outline of the large pines
Thick silhouettes against the late twilight
We keep each other on the path
Until our hands are back on the front doorknob
Where we give glory for all souls and our lives and everything lit
That night before bed
I leave the porch light on

Excerpt from a Birdwatcher's Notebook: Turkey

I drove by the specialized barns
    on the ridge just beyond Bucksnort.

Next to fields of wild strutting toms
    live domestic white birds. Through a gap

I caught glimpses of pink balded tops,
    plump bodies concealed below. Like

their heads were already severed but still
    going about the day. I cringe at their fate.

On a park bench, later, I ponder
    while I eat a cold sandwich for lunch.

Busses of children pass on the highway.

Waiting to Tap the Northern Lights on the Shoulder

Cows bellow in the distance
        A star falls and slashes across my view
I hear the clicks and sings of stretching barbed wire
        as the temperature drops
and an unseen breeze passes by
        Resident owls asking "who cooks for who"
and the coyotes yip beyond sight
        Tonight was supposed to be the night
A swaying aurora on a lonely dirt road
        beside an empty field just north of the Iowa
border unpolluted by mankind or light

Another falling fragment catches my eyes
        Brushing through the darkness
The ground is frozen
        naked to the heavens
ready to surrender
        weightless to the sky

Please come dance with me
        Show me your flair
in this place to heal and feel right
        where nothing else matters
Except the moment we're in
        where meteorites streak
and land in imagination
        Surrender yourself
I'll bare my bones too
        We can achieve the pinnacle of a trinity

Create one from two ones
instead of just two

My mind is on the precipice
When I'm snapped back to my body
as the clock reaches yet another day
nothing changed
The Polaris too shy to perform
The fence speaks, the wind blows
The balance of nature runs through all
I cleanse my breath before I open again
I'm left to wait another night
In that moment I give myself to the world
I was given something in return

Directions to Remember

If I die tomorrow
people might remember
that all my favorites were blue.

Forget this.

Forget that I was funny, and laughed.
That I went to a small school. My degrees
held. That I was a teacher. That I loved
to cook. How I helped others. Pretend
they wouldn't say, "he was always good
for a pour of barrel strength bourbon,
and he could count cribbage hands
before the cards hit the bar." Don't let
people know that I was a sports fan.
That I enjoyed a hard strike or fair hunt.
It doesn't matter that I traveled
and enjoyed a good story. Nature and wild
environments were instrumental
in my development as a human,
an artist, but that is not my epilogue.
You should not listen to hear
that I was a good father, friend, son. Don't
for a moment believe I was a poet.

Even if all of that's true, I want them
to know —want ***YOU*** to know… I cannot
truly be defined by any of those things.
Even folks that don't appreciate
my existence —see the excess.

Because my contemplation is spillage.
My creativity forms foam.
For better or worse, my passion
and emotion emanate, sometimes
beyond control. For I am manifested
by what I cannot contain. If you witnessed
my essence within rip through my skin, I pray
the collateral you see is not damage. Because I am
who I am, and I do what I do, simply
because my heart, whether empty
or full, is too big
to be contained by my body.
Let me leave my physique
and seep into your memory.

Do like this. Do like this —
put your fingers to your wrists.
Feel my beat.
I thump … Your blood … I pump … I'm there.

And ***that*** is what you'll remember.

About the Author

Jake Griggs is a dual citizen (US and Luxembourg) who was born in the Twin Cities and raised all over, before settling in rural Southeastern Minnesota. This is his debut poetry collection. A curious creative, Jake took a circuitous path to writing. A recent graduate of Mankato State's MFA program, he began publishing poetry in 2024. When not hunting, fishing, traveling, or looking for a good game of cribbage, he works as the Dean of Trade and Technology at Minnesota State College Southeast in Winona and Red Wing. Jake resides in the driftless region with his wife and cat.

Acknowledgements

To the Woman at the Front Desk of the Americas Best Value Inn and Suites was originally published in the *Water~Stone Review*, Vol. 28 Fall 2025.

O'Leary Lake was originally published in *RockPaperPoem*, Issue 10, Winter 2024.

Cyrtanthus Ventricosis was originally published by the Lone Mountain Literary Society, in *The Nature of Things*, Issue 3, Spring 2026.

www.ingramcontent.com/pod-product-compliance
Lightning Source LLC
La Vergne TN
LVHW090610110826
845146LV00001B/325

* 9 7 9 8 9 9 4 4 3 1 6 1 0 *